*M*others and daughters have a bond
of closeness that will never break....
The love between them is proof of
love's power.

— Donna Fargo

Blue Mountain Arts®

"The Language of the Heart..." series

The Language of the Heart...

Mothers & Daughters

A Blue Mountain Arts® Collection

Edited by Patricia Wayant

Blue Mountain Press™

Boulder, Colorado

We wish to thank Susan Polis Schutz for permission to reprint the following poems that appear in this publication: "The relationship between a mother…," "There is a fine line…," "Mother, I want to…," and "In good and bad times…." Copyright © 1986, 1987, 1990 by Stephen Schutz and Susan Polis Schutz. All rights reserved.

Library of Congress Control Number: 2019938219
ISBN: 978-1-68088-295-7

◨ and Blue Mountain Press are registered in U.S. Patent and Trademark Office. Certain trademarks are used under license.

Acknowledgments appear on the last page.

Handmade paper used on cover made in Thailand.
Printed and assembled in China.
First Printing: 2019

⊕ Interior of this book is printed on recycled paper.

Blue Mountain Arts, Inc.
P.O. Box 4549, Boulder, Colorado 80306

Contents

(Authors listed in order of first appearance)

Mothers & Daughters

$\mathcal{T}$he love between
a mother and daughter
is a bond of the strongest kind.
It is a love of the present,
interwoven with memories of the past
and dreams of the future.
It is wanting only the best
for each other and wanting to help
anytime there is a need.
It is making time to be together
and knowing just what to do and say.
It is an unconditional,
forever kind of love.

Barbara Cage

When I Look at You, Mother...

I see someone who has been there
for me my entire life,
and I wonder if you know
how wonderful you really are.
How the love in your eyes,
the tenderness in your voice,
the soft, comforting touch of your hands
have healed more wrongs
than any team of specialists could ever heal?
That the place you have created, our home,
is warm and full of life and love?
And how much I appreciate all the love and the care
you put into the hours of everyday life?
Those are special gifts and special talents.
They are not something that
can be taught in school.
They are gifts of love,
gifts that I hope to possess someday
and to be able to share with my family.

 Lea Walsh

In You, Daughter...

I see pieces of me when I look at you —
yet you are completely, uniquely,
beautifully your own person,
and I am so proud of you.

From the light in your eyes
to the warmth of your spirit;
from the way you take on the day
to the joy you create;
your courage in tough times,
your compassion for others,
and the way that you can laugh
and remember what matters...
it's amazing to see the woman
you have become.

 Chinwe I. Ndubuka

Mothers and daughters.

These simple words hold a relationship that is filled with such beauty and complexity that it defies definition. Ask any woman what this relationship means and you'll likely get a long pause in response. Maybe you'll get an intake of breath and a run or two at putting words together. You'll probably get a far-off look as she tries to describe the love, the emotion, the frustration, the joy, the delight, the crazy, the tears, the uncertainties, the excitement, the fears, and the bond she shares with her daughter or her own mother. If a daughter happens to be next to a mother when the question is asked, you can bet the two will look at each other and search each other's faces for the right words to describe their bond. They will take in each other's eyes and expressions and feel a hundred emotions.

This is the mother-daughter relationship.

 Rachel Anne Ridge

$\mathcal{M}$others and daughters have a bond of closeness that will never break — a friendship that's unconditional between two never-ending friends. One is always looking up to the other, and both are looking out for the other. They are perfect listeners, helpers, advisers, hopers, honesty brokers, promise keepers, and dream sharers. The love between them is proof of love's power.

 Donna Fargo

$\mathcal{T}$he bond between a mother and her child is the only real and purest bond in the world, the only true love we can ever find in our lifetime.

 Ama H. Vanniarachchy

Before she was a part of my life, I used to dream about what it would be like to have a daughter.

Scattered among my hopes for someone to love and share things with were many fears of motherhood and all its challenges.

I wondered whether I had it in me to give enough of myself to meet the needs of a tiny new person who would depend on me for everything.

I wondered whether I could love and care for a beautiful daughter the way I imagined in my dreams — completely and without reservations.

When she finally became a part of my life, I knew right away that she was everything I had hoped for and more.

The little fears disappeared in the rush of love I felt, and when I held her in my arms I wanted to stay that way forever.

 Linda Sackett-Morrison

*M*y mother's arms were the first to hug me;
she could make me feel like I was
    the center of her universe
when she wrapped me up in safety,
    security,
and the warmth of belonging.
Her voice was the first to sing to me,
make me smile, and lull me to sleep.
Her hands were the first to nurture me;
she kissed away my fears and comforted me
through colds and fevers
and an endless list of childhood maladies.
Her gentle fingers smoothed my hair
    and soothed my aches and bruises.
She was the first person to encourage me,
cheer me on, give me approval,
and applaud when I did something worthy.
She is the person who taught me
what it means to be loving and loved.

 Patricia A. Teckelt

We're More Than Mother and Daughter... We're Friends

We're not just family, but true friends.
We can confide in each other
no matter what the subject.
We can share laughter and good times,
discuss life's challenges,
try to help fix each other's problems,
or just be there to listen and understand.
We can count on each other
more than anyone else in the world,
knowing we will be there for each other
    under any circumstances.
The love and support we share
provide us with confidence,
courage, and strength
    whenever we need it most.
We're more than mom and daughter...
we're best friends.

Barbara Cage

$\mathcal{I}$ remember how before she was born, I hoped for a daughter. Little did I know then that what I was really hoping for was a friend — someone to laugh with even when life was not funny, someone whose very presence would fill me with a love so deep and pure that I could finally understand what it meant to actually love someone more than I loved myself.

 Lea Walsh

$\mathcal{I}$n life, we are lucky if we can find a best friend whom we can trust and admire and love. But when that friend is also our mother, then we are twice blessed and fortunate beyond our dreams.

Audrey Esar

The relationship between
a mother and daughter
is comprised of a very deep
understanding of and support for
each other
It is based on an enormous
amount of emotion and love
There is no other relationship
in the world
where two women are so much
like one

When I gave birth to
my beautiful daughter
I never knew what a
special relationship
a mother and daughter could have
As she got older
and started to understand more
about being a female
I felt as if I were going through
all the stages of growing up
once again

I felt a strong urge
to protect her from anything
that could possibly hurt her
but I knew that if I did
she would not be prepared
to face the real world
So I tried to
establish the right balance
by showing her and
explaining to her
what I consider to be
the most important things in life

And I have loved her every second
of her life
I have supported her at all times
and as her mother, as a person
and as a friend
I will always continue
to cherish and love
everything about her
my beautiful daughter

 Susan Polis Schutz

There's Something Special About Having a Daughter...

To have a daughter is to feel proud when I wake up each day, to feel peace in my heart, to hear the music of joy and laughter wherever I go, and to walk with pride and happiness in my heart for all we share.

Jacqueline Schiff

Whenever I am in my daughter's presence, I know I am looking at the smiling face of one of the most wonderful people I will ever have the privilege of knowing.

If I could be given any gift imaginable, one that would make me happy beyond words, make me feel truly blessed, and make my days just shine… the gift I'd choose would be her… each and every time.

Terry Bairnson

...and Being a Daughter

I'm blessed and I couldn't be more grateful. Do you want to know why? Because I'm a mother, but that's only half of it. I'm blessed because, when I need to, I can still just be a daughter. I get the feeling that there is nothing more precious than to have both of these roles, simultaneously.

Adrianna Stepiano

A daughter is a mother's gender partner, her closest ally in the family confederacy, an extension of her self. And mothers are their daughters' role model, their biological and emotional road map, the arbiter of all their relationships.

Victoria Secunda

Perfectly... Imperfect

I am not a perfect mother and I will never be. You are not a perfect daughter and you will never be. But put us together and we will be the best mother and daughter we would ever be.

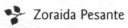 Zoraida Pesante

*L*ife is crazy — a sort of controlled chaos as I try to figure out this thing called parenting. We all have our flaws and that's what makes each of us unique. My daughter has taught me that the little things in life are not important, that embracing each day with passion and exhilaration is the best way to live. She has taught me to let go of my insecurities and has helped me embrace life's blemishes. My daughter has taught me to be comfortable in my own skin. I'm happy being perfectly imperfect, because in my daughter's eyes, I'm Mom... and that's perfection.

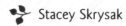 Stacey Skrysak

*M*others and daughters
are two separate worlds
getting to know each other better.
Laughing together, being silly,
trying on each other's heart —
mothers and daughters are
a celebration of living.
They are there for each other
as they go through the ups,
downs, and in-betweens —
    and they thrive.
They have open arms
for each other,
the perfect recipe for
    a happy family,
and all the fun you can
bake into a day.
They are everyday treasures
who grow more beautiful
    through time.
Who can imagine a world
without mothers and daughters?
They are each other's star,
lighting the world
    with their love.

 Linda E. Knight

Learning and Growing Together

Throughout the years, just watching my daughter grow from childhood to adulthood has brought me more pleasure than anyone could know. From her, I have learned that life's most precious gift is the family around us.

 Linda E. Knight

My daughter has enriched my life more than she'll ever know, and she has taught me so much about being a parent, a mom, a friend... and a person.

Debbie Burton-Peddle

$\mathcal{M}$y mother taught me a few important lessons while I was growing up. One was to always be yourself and don't try to pretend to be somebody different. Another was to never be afraid to try new things. And she also instilled in me and my brothers a strong desire to help other people and try to make the world a better place.

 Dolores Huerta

$\mathcal{A}$ mother teaches her daughter how to feel about herself, about handling pressure, about relishing life's joys and conquering fears. She teaches her daughter about true beauty, how to dress up, when to turn on the charm, the importance of trusting God, and how to care for a daughter of her own someday. She teaches her daughter everything she knows about being an independent woman, then gets frustrated beyond belief when her daughter acts like one.

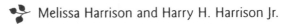 Melissa Harrison and Harry H. Harrison Jr.

Through the Laughter
and the Tears

*F*or each moment of joy a daughter experiences,
there is a silent joy shared by her mother,
along with a silent prayer
of thanks to God for the blessing
He has given her, her child.
Behind each tear shed and each hurt felt,
there is a silent tear and a silent hurt
felt deep inside a mother's heart.

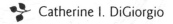 Catherine I. DiGiorgio

I couldn't begin to count the number of times my
mother tolerated my moods, consoled my heartbreaks
and disappointments, endured my ups and downs,
listened to words confused by tears, and just simply
understood for no other reason than because she
loves me.

Susan M. Pavlis

We had some difficult times in our relationship — times when our strong wills overshadowed the love in our hearts. Sometimes I chose a different path than my mother wanted me to, yet she was always there to show me the way back home and to welcome me into her comforting arms.

 Lori Glover

Each different stage in our lives turned another page. My memory recalls them for me: birthday parties, first days of school, holidays, laughter, fun, and even tears. Without a sprinkle of those tears, even a flood of them at times, we could not have appreciated the rainbows, starlight, love, sharing, and caring.

Vicki Silvers

Mother-Daughter Conversation

She calls from a thousand
miles away. Instead of wandering
through our usual thickets
of hello-how-are-you-how-is-your-life
our voices sound light and clear,
without the dim static
of doubt and hesitation.
We ride our telephone horses
toward each other, not stumbling,
not having to dismount and look
for another way in, and she says
you've always been my model
for feminism, for justice; now
you're my role model for compassion
and I can only pause and say
thank you, recalling the tough survival days
and the love that rode through
so many years to arrive, finally, here.

 Maril Crabtree

There were times when we struggled.
She was longing for her own independence
and searching for her own place in the world.
I remember those times as I tried to
hold her close and hold on tightly to my little girl,
knowing all the time in my heart it was a
part of growing up for her and for me,
a part of life we would endure
and that eventually we would become closer
    than ever before.

 Deanna Beisser

I think of what we have been through as a
family — everything, the good and the bad.
From the toughest and most challenging days
to these glorious times, I would change very
little. After struggling and learning, we're all
finding our place in life — purpose, wholeness,
authenticity, fulfillment, love.

I couldn't be more grateful.

Betty DeGeneres

Connected
Heart to Heart

*A*s mothers and daughters, we are connected
with one another. My mother is in the bones of
my spine, keeping me straight and true. She is
in my blood, making sure it runs rich and strong.
She is in the beating of my heart.

I cannot now imagine a life without her.

 Kristin Hannah

*F*rom the time she was born until she was
fifteen, I didn't know where I left off and
she began. We were joined at the hip or
the heart or the brain.

 Lee Grant

Though we're not always together, we always have a strong, warm, and forever feeling of togetherness. It's there in our lives, welcoming us just as surely as the sun coming up in the morning and just as certain as the stars that shine above.

I think that feeling is such a beautiful reflection of the wonderful bond we share, and it says so much about the remarkable and thankful things that two caring souls are capable of.

— S. J. Ellenson

If mothers are the heart of a family, then daughters are its link with the past and the future. Daughters are a reflection of what came before and a vision of what will be. Like their mothers, they will become the caretakers, the archivists, and the enfolding strength of their own families… and the legacy continues.

— Jill Morgan

A Mother Is...

A mother is someone who loves
and is never afraid to show that love.
A mother sometimes pushes aside
    her own needs
to focus on the needs of others.
A mother is a haven of love,
a listening ear when no one else cares
    or has time to listen.
A mother makes time.
A mother gives advice when asked
but always with the understanding
that it is only advice,
leaving her daughter free
to make her own choices.
Though there are some times
when mother and daughter don't agree,
a mother respects her daughter's choices,
encourages her decisions,
and listens to her reasoning.
A mother is all these things
to her daughter, and more.

 Dale Harcombe

A Daughter Is...

A daughter is a little piece
  of yourself
looking back at you.
She is another chance for you
    to realize the dreams
      of your past.
She is God's most precious gift,
    and adventures without end.

A daughter is your best creation.
She's a best friend
    and a fashion adviser.

Only she knows why
    you love purple
      and hate turnips.

A daughter is never-ending love,
    given and received,
and learning to love yourself.
Of all the things that
    happen in life,
      a daughter is the best.

 Brenda A. Morris

Planning the Future

I never dreamed my daughter would be 16
until the day arrived with a car full of kids
and balloons, take-out Mexican food
and a Baskin Robbins ice cream cake.
A few months later and she has a boyfriend
in a baseball cap and baggy pants, two gold hoop
earrings and a shaved head. They are happy.
After school they do their homework together,
stretched out on her bed, the door open
to the edge of the legal limit.
Every history question finished deserves
a kiss. They're embarrassed by the names
they've invented for each other,
by their tenderness. Toward evening

they watch MTV, mute the volume
during the commercials and plan their future —
junior college, then marriage, then kids,
what they'll take with them — his dog,
her rat. I'm happy for them, even knowing
what will happen — the last gift, the last
kiss, her huddled on her bed, blinded
by her own bright pain. And I can see clearly
the day she'll walk away, keys on a ring,
a suitcase banging her legs.
Then the real work of motherhood will begin,
the job of waking into each morning, trusting.

 Dorianne Laux

In My Mother's Footsteps

I remember so long ago when
I followed so closely behind her.
She protected my every move
while holding my hand, and
her love never failed me.
As I grew from year to year,
her hand opened to allow my
reaching out and growth.
She watched me strive and achieve,
with so much pride and silent prayer.
She also let me fail on my own,
but was always there to pick me up
while we shared the tears.

I learned so much from her,
and silently I will always reflect,
with smiles and grateful tears,
upon our moments together.
I realize that I may no longer
follow behind her as I did when I
was small; instead our footsteps
have become equal strides as we
walk side by side, together in friendship.
I don't know if I can ever
repay her for the gifts of life she's given me,
but if I can live my life by giving
to others as much as she has given to me…
I will be following in her footsteps once again.

 Danine Winkler

Raising a Daughter

*A*s one mom said, "Raising a daughter is like growing a flower. You give it your best. If you've done your job well, she blooms. And after that, she leaves."

All moms instinctively know this. Maybe loving someone so much, someone who is so much a part of you, is what makes the mother-daughter relationship so special. Mothers know that love is forever. And that's a lesson their daughters can't wait to pass along.

 Melissa Harrison and Harry H. Harrison Jr.

$\mathcal{M}$y mother's influence is the core of how I parent my own children and, on a broader scale, how I hope to interact with all my family members, my friends, my fans, and every daily encounter along the way. My mother's philosophy for how to approach every interaction, experience, challenge, and choice in every single day was this: "The key is love." She would always, first, strive to "be positive" and, second, to always be kind. If her kindness was rejected for any reason, my mother's solution was to put forth even more kindness.

I know my daily approach to mothering isn't as consistent or as wise as my mom's, but I also know that she would have been the first one to respond to my shortcomings with kindness and some positive words of encouragement. She was always ready with a positive thought for anyone she would talk to, a thought that would always move us forward in our thinking.

Marie Osmond

An Invisible Thread

Unlike the mother-son relationship, a daughter's relationship with her mother is something akin to bungee diving. She can stake her claim in the outside world in what *looks* like total autonomy — in some cases, even "divorce" her mother in a fiery exit from the family — but there is an invisible emotional cord that snaps her back. For always there is the memory of mother whose judgments are so completely absorbed into the daughter's identity that she may wonder where Mom leaves off and she begins.

 Victoria Secunda

Like one, like the other.
Like daughter, like mother.

Author Unknown

Sometimes when I look in the mirror,
I see my mother's face.
I wonder if she sees me
when she looks in the mirror.

Sometimes when I hear myself talk to my daughter,
I think I sound like my mother.
I wonder if the words coming out of my mouth
are hers or mine.

Sometimes when my daughter is sick or hurting,
I touch her cheek or put my arms
    around her shoulder.
I wonder how it's possible for a mother
to ever let go of her child.

Sometimes the lines between us are so blurred
and the connections so strong.
I wonder if there's not an invisible thread
    tying us together...
my mother, my daughter, and me.

 Anna Marie Edwards

Always There for Each Other

*W*e all hope to feel our mother's arm around our shoulders when we're worried, to feel it gently let go when life calms down. It's an intricate duet that moms and daughters dance — one backing off when the other needs space, moving up close when the unfamiliar threatens.

❧ Cathie Kryczka

*I*n my mother's arms, I've found
    comfort from the world so many times —
from fears, hurts, and everything
    that troubles me.
I know that if anything happens
    to bother me now,
those arms are always open
    just for me.

❧ Barbara J. Hall

*D*aughter, your eyes told me every day that even if no one else in this world ever needed me, you always would. You could look into my eyes and assure me that we would grow together and become best friends, and that's just what we did.

 Debra Heintz Cavataio

*J*f my life is sane and if it's full, it's in large measure because I have such a remarkable daughter.

 Ruth Bader Ginsburg

Of course I always knew
that someday my daughter would be
a woman building her own life,
chasing dreams she's spent
     years creating.
She would sit across from me
and smile that smile
that would remind me of when
she was a little girl.
A million memories
would pass through my mind,
and I would be so proud
of who she's become
and so very thankful
to have been blessed with
a daughter like her.

 Kellie L. McCracken

$\mathcal{N}$ow that I'm grown, I realize
that all the wise decisions my mother
made over the years have helped me
become the person I am.
The love, the trust, the discipline,
and the understanding she gave me
were exactly what I needed to grow.
I find that I appreciate her
even more than I did when I was little,
because I know now what
a difficult job it is to be
the kind of mother she is.
And even though I'm not little anymore,
I still come to her to talk, laugh,
and maybe even cry about the way
this world can be.
At this time in my life,
I need and love her more than ever.

 — Sharon Johnson O'Donnell

Letting Go

Letting go is not easy. But when I look at my daughter now — a beautiful young woman, strong in her convictions and determined to face life on her own terms — I feel my heart swell with pride and joy...

In one simple truth: even though her hand may slip away from mine, we will hold each other in our hearts forever.

— Nancy Gilliam

It was hard when you went away —
for how was I to know
the serendipity of letting go
would be seeing you come home again
and meeting in a new way
woman to woman —
friend to friend.

— Marilee Zdenek

There is a fine line between
a mother telling her daughter
too much
or too little
I hope I have struck a proper balance
I have always wanted to tell you
how honored I am that you
seek out my opinions
I appreciate the trust you have in me
I also want to tell you that
I have an immense trust in you
and I am very proud of you
as I watch you growing up to be an
intelligent, independent, sensitive person

 Susan Polis Schutz

If We Had It to Do All Over Again...

Daughter, there are things I did
when you were young that I would do differently now.
I am stronger and wiser than I was then,
and I wish we could relive those times
   and give you a perfect childhood.
But in spite of my shortcomings,
and perhaps because of those difficult times,
you have become a fine, strong young woman,
   and I am so proud of you.

It is wonderful to be able to talk to you as a friend,
and to see you radiate the love and understanding
that is the most important aspect of our relationship.
I marvel at your wisdom and the depth of your perception.
I am thankful that I can let go,
knowing that you will stand on your own
and become more self-assured each day.

It's wonderful to know that we can now
be supportive of each other as equals.
I value your insight, and I treasure the bond we share.
I may not be able to undo the things I wish I could,
but I can be forever thankful that
the things I hold most dear — honesty, love, integrity —
   are alive and well in you.

❧ Judy McKee Howser

$\mathcal{M}$other, I want to apologize
for any problems
that I may have caused you
in the past
I am not
the easiest person
to live with
since I am so
independent and strong
but you can be sure
that though it possibly
didn't seem like it
your values and ideals
did pass on to me
and I carry them forward
in all that I do
You always were someone
stable, strong, giving and warm
an ideal person to look up to
This has given me the
strength to lead
my own life
according to my own standards
Your leadership and love
have enabled me to grow
into a very happy person
and I think that is
what every mother wishes
for her daughter

 Susan Polis Schutz

When a Daughter Becomes a Mother

*F*or so many years, I couldn't even imagine
my daughter having a child!
It seemed as though the best thing
I could do for her was to take care of her.
I know I fought her independence for a while,
because I enjoyed raising her so much.
I realize now, though,
that giving a daughter her independence
is the greatest show of love a mother can offer,
because it gives that daughter the opportunity
to realize the joys of motherhood for herself.

My grandchildren are among my greatest joys,
and I am so proud of my daughter —
not only for having a child,
but for being a wonderful mother.
She has taught me that
the happiness she gives me now
is as great as the happiness she gave me
when she was a little girl —
it's just different…
in a very wonderful way.

❧ Vicki Perkins

$\mathcal{I}$ am in no rush to have children of my own, but when I do, I can only hope I have a daughter who can grow into a friend. I hope I can foster the same kind of relationship my mother did with me. And I sincerely hope that one day, when I look in the mirror, I see somebody like my mother.

 Caitlin Attal

$\mathcal{I}$n the wild, an elephant mother and daughter stay in close proximity their whole lives; I hope I am that lucky.

Jodi Picoult

For My
Grown-Up Daughter

It seems like yesterday
I tucked you in at night,
whispering a prayer of thanks
for another day of
having you in my life.
Not so long ago,
we were putting your baby teeth
out for the tooth fairy
and reading storybooks
until you fell asleep in my arms.
It felt as though you grew overnight
into a beautiful young lady.
Today I see you reaching out to people,
showing that one person
can make a difference in this world.

And what a difference you've made!
I know my life could never have been so
full and complete without your being
such an important part of it.
I've watched the difference you've made
in the lives of others as well.
You have a very special gift
that inspires people to be
the best they can be.
I'm so proud of all that you do,
and I hope you'll never forget that
I love you with all my heart!

 Carol Was

A Mother Wants Her Daughter to Know...

In good and bad times
I will love you
and no matter
what you do
   or how you think
or what you say
   you can depend on
my support, guidance
   friendship and love
every minute of every day
I love being your mother

 Susan Polis Schutz

A Daughter Wants Her Mother to Remember...

I've looked up to you all my life;
growing up, I assumed
   you could do most anything.
The pride I have in you goes beyond
all the things you have done.
I'm proud of the person
   you've always been —
kind, caring, dependable, and wise.
I'm proud you are my mom!

 Cheryl Barker

Mothers and Daughters Share an Exceptional Love

The love between mothers and daughters is one of life's most precious gifts. It is a bond that will never break.

There may be arguments along the way, but they never last very long. There may be tears, but they are always cleared away with a smile.

Theirs is an unconditional love that is not just based on family; it is born out of the best kind of friendship.

Mothers and daughters share in the joy of every memory and appreciate every bit of their history together as well as their dreams for tomorrow. They love each other in the most exceptional way.

— Mary Guindon

$\mathcal{W}$hat I treasure most is the love that has grown between us. Maybe it's because we have grown in our own ways and in our own times to be more receptive to what is really important in our lives.

 Elizabeth Hornsey Reeves

$\mathcal{N}$othing could warm my
heart more than knowing that
the beautiful bond between the
two of us will always be…
one of the sweetest blessings
anyone could ever receive.

 Marin McKay

Acknowledgments

We gratefully acknowledge the permission granted by the following authors, publishers, and authors' representatives to reprint poems or excerpts in this publication: PrimaDonna Entertainment Corp. for "Mothers and daughters have a bond..." by Donna Fargo. Copyright © 2008 by PrimaDonna Entertainment Corp. All rights reserved. Harvest House Publishers for "Mothers and daughters. These simple..." from WITH LOVE, MOM by Dawn Camp, foreword by Rachel Anne Ridge. Copyright © 2018 by Rachel Anne Ridge. All rights reserved. Ama H. Vanniarachchy for "The bond between a mother and her child...." Copyright © 2019 by Ama H. Vanniarachchy. All rights reserved. Adrianna Stepiano for "I'm blessed and I couldn't...." Copyright © 2019 by Adrianna Stepiano. All rights reserved. Dell Publishing, an imprint of Random House, a division of Penguin Random House LLC, for "A daughter is a mother's..." and "Unlike the mother-son relationship..." from WOMEN AND THEIR FATHERS by Victoria Secunda. Copyright © 1992 by Victoria Secunda. All rights reserved. Zoraida Pesante for "I am not a perfect mother...." Copyright © 2019 by Zoraida Pesante. All rights reserved. Stacey Skrysak for "Life is crazy — a sort of..." from "I'm Happy Being Perfectly Imperfect," *Mamalode*, December 30, 2016, http://mamalode.com/story/toddlers-pre-school/im-happy-being-perfectly-imperfect/. Copyright © 2016 by Stacey Skrysak. All rights reserved. Linda E. Knight for "Mothers and daughters...." Copyright © 2019 by Linda E. Knight. All rights reserved. Dolores Huerta Foundation for "My mother taught me..." by Dolores Huerta from WHAT I TOLD MY DAUGHTER, edited by Nina Tassler with Cynthia Littleton. Copyright © 2016 by Dolores Huerta. All rights reserved. Workman Publishing Company, Inc., for "A mother teaches her..." and "As one mom said..." from MOTHER TO DAUGHTER by Melissa Harrison & Harry H. Harrison Jr. Copyright © 2005, 2013 by Melissa Harrison & Harry H. Harrison Jr. All rights reserved. Maril Crabtree for "Mother-Daughter Conversation," *Literary Mama*, May 2017, http://www.literarymama.com/poetry/archives/2017/05/mother-daughter-conversation.html. Copyright © 2017 by Maril Crabtree. All rights reserved. HarperCollins Publishers for "I think of what we have been through..." from LOVE, ELLEN by Betty DeGeneres. Copyright © 1999 by Betty DeGeneres. All rights reserved. Crown Books, an imprint of Random House, a division of Penguin Random House LLC, and Jane Rotrosen Literary Agency for "As mothers and daughters..." from SUMMER ISLAND: A NOVEL by Kristin Hannah. Copyright © 2001 by Kristin Hannah. All rights reserved. Signet, an imprint of Penguin Publishing Group, a division of Penguin Random House LLC, for "If mothers are the heart..." from MOTHERS AND DAUGHTERS: CELEBRATING THE GIFT OF LOVE WITH 12 NEW STORIES edited by Jill Morgan. Compilation copyright © 1998 by Jill Morgan, Martin Greenberg, and Robert Weinberg. All rights reserved. The Permissions Company, LLC, on behalf of BOA Editions, Ltd., www.boaeditions.org, for "Planning the Future" from WHAT WE CARRY by Dorianne Laux. Copyright © 1994 by Dorianne Laux. All rights reserved. Berkley, an imprint of Penguin Publishing Group, a division of Penguin Random House LLC, and William Morris Endeavor Entertainment LLC for "My mother's influence is the core..." from THE KEY IS LOVE: A MOTHER'S WISDOM, A DAUGHTER'S GRATITUDE by Marie Osmond. Copyright © 2013 by Marie Inc. All rights reserved. Rogers Media for "We all hope to feel..." from "Mothers and Daughters" by Cathie Kryczka. Copyright © 2001 by Rogers Media. All rights reserved. HarperCollins Christian Publishing for "It was hard when you..." from SPLINTERS IN MY PRIDE by Marilee Zdenek. Copyright © 1979 by Marilee Zdenek. All rights reserved. The Thought & Expression Company, LLC, for "I am in no rush..." from "5 Reasons Why I Know My Mother Is My Best Friend" by Caitlin Attal, *Thought Catalog*, March 19, 2014, https://www.thoughtcatalog.com/caitlin-attal/2014/03/5-reasons-why-i-know-my-mother-is-my-best-friend/. Copyright © 2014 by Caitlin Attal. All rights reserved. Ballantine Books, an imprint of Random House, a division of Penguin Random House LLC, and Hodder and Stoughton Limited for "In the wild, an elephant mother..." from LEAVING TIME: A NOVEL by Jodi Picoult. Copyright © 2014 by Jodi Picoult. All rights reserved.

A careful effort has been made to trace the ownership of selections used in this anthology in order to obtain permission to reprint copyrighted material and give proper credit to the copyright owners. If any error or omission has occurred, it is completely inadvertent, and we would like to make corrections in future editions provided that written notification is made to the publisher:

BLUE MOUNTAIN ARTS, INC., P.O. Box 4549, Boulder, Colorado 80306